BOOKS BY JOAN ELMA RAHN

Grocery Store Botany
How Plants Are Pollinated
How Plants Travel
Seeing What Plants Do
More About What Plants Do
Alfalfa, Beans & Clover
Grocery Store Zoology
The Metric System
Seven Ways to Collect Plants

*

SEVEN WAYS
TO COLLECT
PLANTS

---

*

SEVEN WAYS
TO COLLECT
PLANTS

by Joan Elma Rahn

WITH ILLUSTRATIONS

PREPARED BY THE AUTHOR

Atheneum   New York

*   *1978*   *

Library of Congress Cataloging in Publication Data

Rahn, Joan Elma
Seven ways to collect plants.

SUMMARY: Discusses ways to collect and preserve
plants and several techniques to produce
prints and photographs of the collection.
1. Plants—Collection and preservation—Juvenile
literature.   2. Plant prints—Juvenile literature.
3. Photography of plants—Juvenile literature.
[1. Plants—Collection and preservation.   2. Plant
prints.   3. Photography of plants]   I. Title.
QK61.R33   579   77-21181
ISBN 0-689-30640-7

Contents

Introduction   3

1 · Making Leaf Prints with Ink   12

2 · Making Leaf Prints by Xerography   24

3 · Collecting Plants Already Dry   32

4 · Drying Plants   41

5 · Pressing Fresh Plants   54

6 · Collecting Live Plants   65

7 · Photographing Plants   75

*

SEVEN WAYS
TO COLLECT
PLANTS

---

*

Introduction

Wherever you live, there probably are hundreds of different kinds of plants. Getting to know them can be interesting. And one of the best ways of doing this is collecting them—the whole plants or perhaps just their leaves or flowers or seeds or fruits. You can make prints from the leaves. You can preserve plants by drying them or pressing them. You can collect live plants to grow in a garden, and if you have a camera, you can photograph them.

Whatever you choose to do, when you collect plants, remember that some of our wild flowers are becoming rare. In many places you are not permitted to pick rare and endangered plants. Even if there is no law against it, it still is something you should not do. Usually you can get a list of the endangered species in your area from a natural history museum, from the ranger or naturalist at a state park or a national park, or from organiaztions interested in wildlife. Your science teacher may have a list or may be able to help you get one.

About the only time it would be right to pick an endangered plant is when you know it will be killed anyway because someone is going to build a house or a store or a road where the plant now grows.

Even if the plants you collect are not rare or endangered, don't be greedy. One or two examples of wild plants should be enough. Some plants that once were abundant became rare because people picked too many of them.

When you collect plants, you will usually want them to be as fresh as possible when you use them. If you take plants from your own backyard, this is no problem, for you can pick them just before you plan to use them. If you are going to take a long walk or travel by car, then you will have to bring something to carry them in. Containers with tight plastic lids, like some cottage cheese cartons, are good. So are plastic food bags.

Whatever type of container you use, put a damp

paper towel in each one before you start out. Soak the paper towel first in water. Then wring just barely enough water out of it so that it is no longer drippy and put it in the container. The wet towel will keep the air around the plants damp but will not form puddles in the bottom of the container. Most plants will stay fresh for several hours this way.

If you use the plastic bags, after you put the plant inside, try to close the bag with as much air trapped inside it. To do this, set it down, hold it wide open, grasp it near the top, and twist the fastener around it. The bag will be plump—a little like a balloon. When you use several bags, this will help to keep the plants from crushing those in other bags. Of course, this will not work if you place something very heavy on a bag. Also, like a balloon, the bag will loose air slowly.

Try to keep the plants in the shade as much as possible, because the closed containers will heat up quickly in direct sunshine, and the plants will wilt. This is especially important when you travel in a car in hot weather.

If you collect dry plant materials in autumn—like dried grasses or Queen Anne's lace—you can just carry these in an open paper bag. There is no need to keep them damp. In fact, dampness might cause them to become moldy.

As you collect plants you can learn a great deal about them—the different kinds of leaves or flowers or fruits they have, what time of year they bloom or set seed. You may notice that many plants grow only in certain places—shady or sunny, wet or dry, gardens and lawns or undisturbed woodlands. Perhaps you will notice relationships between plants and animals. If bees visit the flowers to collect pollen or nectar, perhaps they also pollinate them and so make it more likely that they will produce seed and fruit. Birds or squirrels may help to disseminate seeds as they eat fruits. If you are interested in plants, you probably can learn something every time you observe them.

Introduction

To make your collection a little more valuable, keep a record of the name of the plant (if you know it or can find it) and the date and the place you collected it. If you make leaf prints or press plants, you can put the information on the sheet of paper with the print or the plant. If you take photographs, you can write on the back of the picture or on the cardboard mount for transparencies.

The following list contains some books that can help you to identify the plants you find. Your public library probably has at least some of them and others as well. It may have books about the plants in your state, your county, or your city. An asterisk (*) indicates that the book is available as a relatively inexpensive paperback. A distribution map is a map shaded to show where a particular plant grows.

Wild Flowers and Ferns

DIETZ, MARJORIE J. *The Concise Encyclopedia of Favorite Wild Flowers*. N.Y.: Weathervane Books, 1965.

This book describes one hundred wild flowers and

gives directions for transplanting them to the garden. Since this book was written some of these wild flowers—like orchids, trilliums, and jack-in-the-pulpits—have become quite rare in many areas and probably should not be transplanted.

DURAND, HERBERT. *Field Book of Common Ferns* (Revised edition). N.Y.: G. P. Putnam's Sons, 1949.

This little book contains descriptions of fifty different ferns and four club mosses and directions for growing ferns both indoors and outdoors. It is illustrated with black and white photographs and line drawings.

HYLANDER, CLARENCE J. *The Macmillan Wild Flower Book*. N.Y.: Macmillan Publishing Co., 1954.

The most common wild flowers are described and illustrated with paintings.

RICKETT, HAROLD WILLIAM. *Wild Flowers of the United States*. N.Y.: McGraw-Hill Book Company, 1966.

This is a set of several large books containing color photographs of almost every species of wild flower in the United States.

*Venning, Frank. *Cacti.* N.Y.: Golden Press, 1974.
People living in desert areas probably will get the most use from this book, but at least a few cactuses grow in dry areas throughout most of the United States. This book includes cacti from Central and South America. Illustrated with paintings.

*Zim, Herbert S., and Alexander C. Martin. *Flowers.* N.Y.: Golden Press, 1950.
This book contains paintings and descriptions of some of the most common wild flowers in the United States. Distribution maps.

Weeds

*Spencer, Edwin Rollin. *All About Weeds.* N.Y.: Dover Publications, Inc., 1974.
Some of the most common weeds are described and illustrated with line drawings.

*U.S. Department of Agriculture. *Common Weeds of the United States.* N.Y.: Dover Publications, Inc. 1971.
All important weeds are described. Line drawings

show nearly all parts of the plants in detail. Distribution maps.

Trees

*Brockman, C. Frank. *Trees of North America*. N.Y.: Golden Press, 1968.

The trees of the United States and Canada are described, and paintings show details of leaves, flowers, fruits, or cones. Distribution maps.

Preston, Richard J., Jr. *North American Trees*, 3rd edition. Ames, Iowa: Iowa State University Press, 1976.

This book describes the trees of the United States and Canada except the tropical species in the southernmost part of the United States. Line drawings show leaves, flowers, and fruits. Distribution maps.

When professional botanists arrange their collections, they never mix different kinds of plants on the same sheet or in the same box. That way there is no problem about what label was meant to go with a certain specimen. It also makes it easier if they ever want to change their arrangement or just take out certain kinds of plants.

Of course, you do not have to make that kind of collection. If you have artistic talent you can produce some beautiful decorations by combining parts of different plants into one arrangement. Only your imagination will limit what you can do. You can use leaf prints from different plants to make designs or pictures lovely enough to be framed. You can do the same thing with small pressed flowers and leaves. Bouquets can have any combination of dried flowers. Any of these arrangements would make a nice gift.

1

Making Leaf Prints with Ink

One of the easiest plant collections to make is one of leaf prints. All you need is a stamp pad, a supply of paper, a pair of tweezers, and any leaves that interest you.

For making leaf prints a large stamp pad is easier to use to use than a small one, but even a small one will do. The paper should be the kind that absorbs ink well. Mimeograph paper is best, but most kinds of typing paper work very well, too. Do not use smooth, shiny paper.

Collect some leaves just before you want to use them. Try to choose leaves that are smaller than the stamp pad, for they are easier to handle than large ones. You will have to ink larger leaves one part at a time.

Place each leaf on the stamp pad and cover it with a piece of paper (an old, used piece is fine for this purpose). Rub your fingers over the paper. Be sure you press down on all parts of the leaf—especially its edges. Press gently but firmly.

Materials necessary for making leaf prints.

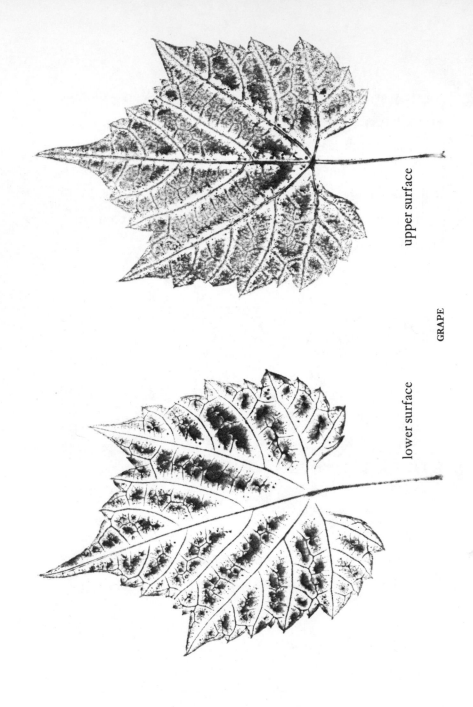

upper surface

lower surface

GRAPE

Then, using the tweezers, pick up the leaf and place it, inked side down, on a piece of clean paper. Again cover it with a piece of scrap paper. Rub the leaf as you did before.

Remove the scrap paper and the leaf. On the good paper you will see the outline of the leaf and the pattern of its veins. The veins of many leaves stand out more on the lower surface than the upper surface. So prints made from the two sides may not be the same.

Smooth, waxy leaves and hairy, fuzzy leaves do not make good prints. Neither do curly leaves. Some leaves will not lie flat when they are very fresh. Letting them wilt a little may help. However, badly wilted leaves are difficult to handle.

You might like to collect prints of as many different leaf types as you can. Here are some examples:

Privet and lilac leaves have *smooth* edges. Their shapes are different, however. Privet leaves are oval, and lilac leaves are pointed at the tip.

The leaves of American elm and catnip have *toothed* edges. Teeth may have sharp, pointed tips—as in elm—or they may be rounded—as in catnip.

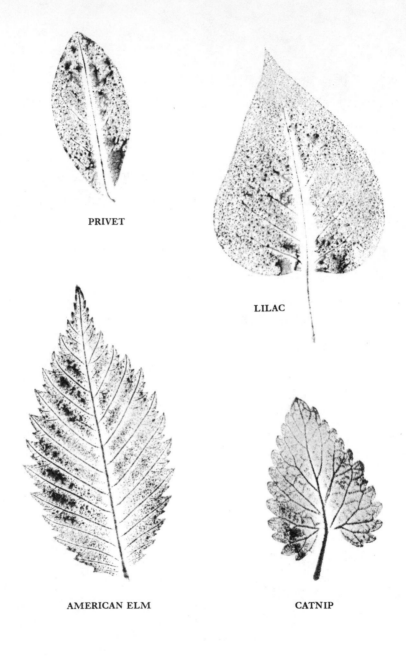

PRIVET

LILAC

AMERICAN ELM

CATNIP

WHITE OAK

SILVER MAPLE

Some leaves, like those of silver maple and white oak, have *lobes*. Lobes are something like teeth, but they are larger and usually there are only a few lobes on a leaf. The edges of a lobe may be smooth—as in white oak—or they may have teeth—as in silver maple.

The lobes of a leaf usually are in one of two arrangements: *palmate* or *pinnate*. In a palmate arrangement, the lobes point outward from just one point in the leaf—similar to your fingers pointing away from the palm of your hand. Silver maple has palmate lobing. In a pinnate arrangement, the lobes point outward from a line—as in a feather. In fact, *pinna* is the Latin work for feather. White oak has pinnate lobing.

Ginkgo has a *fan-shaped* leaf, and nasturtium has a *circular* leaf. These are not common leaf shapes.

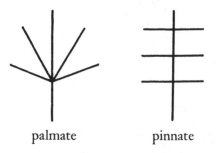

palmate   pinnate

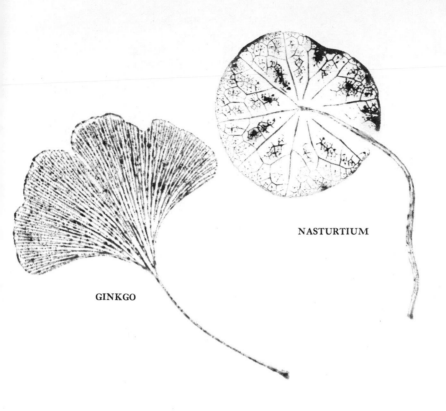

NASTURTIUM

GINKGO

Grasses have long, linear leaves. Some of them have leaves much longer and narrower than the timothy leaf shown here. Actually, only part of the timothy leaf is in the illustration. Grass leaves have a base called a *leaf sheath*. The leaf sheath curls tightly around the stem. You can remove a leaf sheath from the stem, but most of them cannot be flattened enough to make a good leaf print.

*   19   *

TIMOTHY

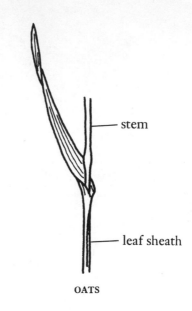

stem

leaf sheath

OATS

CINQUEFOIL

STRAWBERRY

ELDER

Some leaves are *compound*. Compound leaves are divided into several *leaflets*. Like lobes, the leaflets may be in either a palmate or pinnate arrangement. The cinquefoil leaf is palmately compound, and the elder leaf is pinnately compound. A leaf with three leaflets—like the strawberry leaf—is called *trifoliate*. In your collecting you probably will find compound leaves in which the leaflets have smooth edges, toothed edges, or lobes.

In some plants the leaves are all very much alike. In others—like bittersweet nightshade—the leaves have different shapes. Sometimes you will find that the leaves on a single twig are all different from each other.

These leaf types shown here are not all there are. With just a little searching you will find variations on these and perhaps some new ones as well.

2

Making Leaf Prints by Xerography

There is a second way to make leaf prints that is a little more expensive than inking them. You can copy the leaves themselves in xerography machines. Most people call them Xerox machines, but machines made by several different companies can be used.

Some of these machines are good only for making silhouettes of leaves. Others show the patterns of the veins well. You may have to try different machines to find one that makes good leaf prints. Some machines even copy three-dimensional objects such as flowers and fruits. Of

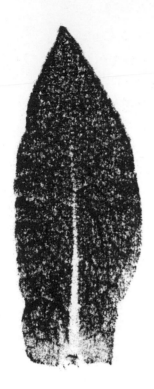
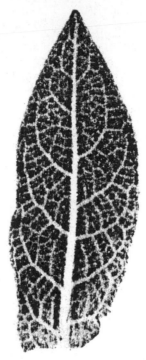

upper surface   lower surface

GREAT MULLEIN LEAVES

course, you must use the kind of machine that will copy from books—not the kind into which you can only insert a sheet to be copied.

As with inked prints, xerography prints made from the two sides of a leaf may look different. Remember that the machine makes a copy of the side you place against the glass. So if you want to copy the lower surface, be sure that the lower surface is against the glass. If some leaves or fruits overlap others, you must try to imagine how they will look from below, for it will be the opposite of what you see from above.

Xerography is a good way to make prints of things that don't make good ink prints—like the fuzzy leaves of great mullein or the waxy, needle-shaped leaves of pine.

Doubly compound leaves, like those of Queen Anne's lace, may also be a little awkward to ink. In doubly compound leaves, the leaflets are divided into still smaller leaflets that make the leaf look lacy.

BUNDLE OF SCOTCH PINE NEEDLES

QUEEN ANNE'S LACE LEAF

Flat objects, like leaves or some twigs, can be laid on the machine and covered with the machine's own cover—just as you would cover any printed page that you want to copy.

If you are copying things that are thick, like flowers, fruits, or some twigs, don't crush them with the machine's cover. Instead, take along a piece of white paper and use that. If you don't cover the specimen, then the background in the print probably will turn out black. Because most leaves and many flowers are also going to appear black, then everything will look too dark—although once in a while you may get an interesting print that looks like a photograph taken by moonlight.

There is at least one occasion, however, when using no cover will produce a better print—when you copy white or light-colored specimens. They will stand out much more clearly against a black background than a white one.

When you work with plant specimens there is always the chance that petals, pollen, dried leaves, or other debris will fall on the machine. So be polite and take along some

SUNFLOWER

paper towels for cleaning up after you have finished. It would also be a good idea to check before making a print to see if you dropped anything while making an earlier one. Anything lying on the glass will show up in your next print.

3

Collecting Plants Already Dry

The easiest way to make a collection of dried plants is to pick those that are already dried naturally. In autumn, a number of grasses and other roadside plants, like Queen Anne's lace, sunflowers, evening primroses, cattails, teasels, and sumac, become dry. Some people collect them at this time to use in winter bouquets. Kept indoors, these dried plants will last all winter. If they are well taken care of, they will last several years. You can use your own imagination for arranging bouquets.

Dry plants should be collected in dry weather. If you

must pick them when they are wet from rain, find a place where you can hang them upside down to let them dry— like a clothesline or some hooks in the attic or basement. An attic is especially good, because attics are usually dry. If you have no attic or basement, lay a yardstick over the backs of two chairs in an out-of-the-way place and hang the plants from it.

This is also a good way to dry plants if you pick them a little early in the season when they are still green. Of course, if you pick them too early, they may not dry well this way.

In autumn many plants have dried fruits and seeds. Instead of making bouquets, you might like to collect the fruits or seeds. You can keep them in shoeboxes or other small cardboard boxes. Label each box with the name of the plant or plants inside.

Egg cartons are good for keeping tiny seeds. Put different seeds in the depressions for the eggs and write the names of the seeds on the inside of the cover. It is easy to tip an egg carton over, so be careful when handling one or the seeds inside are likely to become mixed up.

You probably can also find small containers that someone in the family is about to throw out: old pill bottles, old cosmetic jars, the plastic containers for 35-mm film or fishing lures, and so on.

There are two main types of fruits: *fleshy fruits* and *dry fruits*. Some of each type are good to eat, and some are not. Except for a few special seedless varieties, fruits all contain one or several seeds.

Fleshy fruits are soft and more or less juicy. When you think of fruit to eat for dessert or for a snack, it is fleshy fruits that you probably have in mind—like apples, grapes, oranges, bananas, or watermelons. Most fleshy fruits do not dry well. If they are not eaten by animals first, they either decay or shrivel up. Only some very small fleshy fruits may dry well.

Dry fruits are dry and usually hard or papery when they ripen. You probably haven't thought of many of them as fruits, for we call some of them vegetables, and some are nuts. Bean and pea pods, for example, are dry fruits. We usually eat them when they are still green, but if you let them remain on the plants until they ripen fully, the pods will become dry and papery.

Dry fruits come in two main types: those that split open and those that don't.

To *dehisce* (de HISS) means to split open, so dry fruits that split open are called *dehiscent* (de HISS ent) fruits. Dry fruits that do not split open are called *indehiscent* (IN de HISS ent) fruits.

Dehiscent fruits usually have many seeds inside them. The opening, or dehiscing, of these fruits lets the seeds out. Once they are out, the seeds may become scattered by wind or animals.

The kinds of dehiscent fruits are follicles, legumes, siliques, and capsules.

A *follicle* opens by a slit down one side, and the seeds escape through the slit. Milkweed flowers produce one or two follicles. Columbine flowers produce about five follicles.

A *legume* is a little like a follicle, but it opens by two slits. In some legumes the two sides twist rapidly and scatter the seeds. Tick trefoil, sweet pea, and many others members of the bean family produce legumes.

A *silique* opens when its two sides separate, but there is a wall between them that holds the seeds, which fall

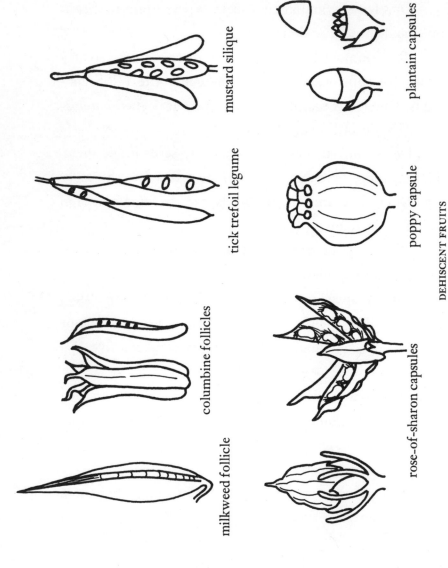

mustard silique

plantain capsules

tick trefoil legume

poppy capsule

columbine follicles

rose-of-sharon capsules

milkweed follicle

DEHISCENT FRUITS

later. Cabbage and other members of the mustard family produce siliques. Some of them have shapes much different from the one illustrated here, but they all have the wall down the center.

A *capsule* has two or more chambers inside it—often three or five. Each has its own seeds. Many capsules, like those of rose of Sharon, open by slits down the length of the capsule—one slit for each chamber. Some capsules, like poppy capsules, have pores—again, one for each chamber. A few capsules open by a slit that runs across the capsule and removes its top. Plantain and purslane, two very common weeds, have tiny capsules that open this way.

If you pick dehiscent fruits when they are still closed but just about to open, they may open later in your boxes.

Indehiscent fruits usually have only one seed inside them. It does not matter that indehiscent fruits do not open, for with only one seed inside, there is no need for scattering. When the seed germinates, the young seedling breaks through both the seed and the fruit. Because so many indehiscent fruits look like seeds, many persons call them just that.

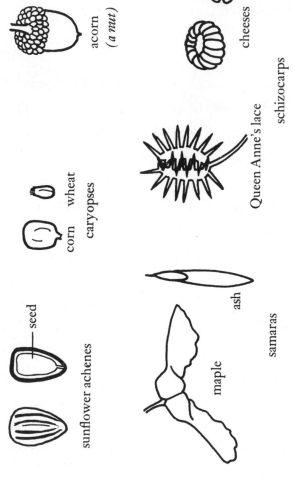

acorn
(*a nut*)

cheeses

schizocarps

wheat
caryopses

corn

Queen Anne's lace

seed

ash

sunflower achenes

samaras

maple

INDEHISCENT FRUITS

The types of indehiscent fruits are achenes, caryopses (grains), nuts, samaras, and schizocarps.

An *achene* contains only one seed, and the seed inside it is loose except where it is attached to the achene wall by its stalk. Sunflower "seeds" are achenes.

A *caryopsis* is like an achene, but the seed inside is attached to the caryopsis wall. You cannot remove the seed from a caryopsis as easily as you can the seed from a sunflower achene. Corn, wheat, and other cereal grains and grasses have caryopses.

A *nut* is like an achene, but it has a hard wall. Acorns are the nuts of oak trees. Walnuts, hickory nuts, beechnuts, and chestnuts are all nuts, but a peanut is not. A peanut is a legume that does not split open.

A *samara* is like an achene, but it has a wing that helps it to be blown away by the wind. Ash trees have samaras. Each maple flower forms two samaras attached to each other that may break apart.

A *schizocarp* is a fruit that splits into two or more fruits, each one like an achene. A Queen Anne's lace schizocarp splits into two spiny fruits. Caraway "seeds" are schizocarps; they usually have separated by the time you buy them in the store. The weed called cheeses has schizocarps that split into many individual fruits; the entire schizocarp looks like a miniature circular cheese cut into pieces.

Dry cones also make an interesting collection. Depending on where you live, you could collect them from pine, spruce, hemlock, fir, redwood, cypress, juniper, or others. They range in size from hemlock cones, some of which are only a half inch long, to some sugar pine cones which are well over a foot in length.

The western part of the United States is especially rich in different kinds of cone-bearing trees. Very few such trees grow naturally in the Great Plains, but even there they are planted as ornamental trees, and cut trees or their branches are brought in for Christmas decorations. Check your library for books that will help you to identify cones from trees growing in your area.

If you collect cones while they are still closed, they probably will open as they dry and release their seeds.

4

Drying Plants

Many plants do not dry attractively in autumn. Instead, their leaves drop off, and so do most of their flower parts. There are ways, however, of drying many of these plants to preserve them. The methods used are intended primarily for flowers, but leaves may often be preserved this way, too. Making bouquets of dried flowers has become a popular hobby.

Flowers to be dried should be picked when they are fresh and healthy-looking. It usually is better to take them when they have opened not quite all the way. If they have passed the peak of condition, the petals soon will be wilting or turning brown or falling.

Although flowers should be fresh when you pick them, they should not be wet. The best time to pick them is about noon on a sunny day. Then any dew that may have formed on them the night before will have evaporated. If you wait until late afternoon, the flowers may begin to wilt, especially on a hot day.

Some flowers open only at one time of day, and you will have to pick them then, no matter what time it is.

If you must pick flowers that are wet, let them stand with their stems in water until the water on the flowers has evaporated. You can help to speed the process by patting them gently with a paper towel.

The reason that the flowers should not have water on them is that you are going to cover them with a *drying agent*, which must be dry so that it can absorb most of the water from inside the flowers. Every bit of water that gets into the drying agent makes it less efficient. Furthermore, wherever there is a drop of water on the flower, the drying agent will cling to the petals and leave a spot there.

There are several different kinds of drying agent you can use. They are all powdery or in the form of fine pellets. One of the best and one of the most popular drying agents is *silica gel*, which is sold in many craft shops and florist's shops. It is rather expensive, but you can use it over and over. However, if you plan to dry many flowers at the same time, you will have to buy a great deal of it at once.

Some less expensive drying agents are borax and yellow corn meal. Some persons use just one of them, others use a mixture. One good recipe for an inexpensive drying agent is:

2 cups of borax
2 cups of yellow corn meal
3 tablespoons of uniodized salt

Mix the ingredients well.

Whatever drying agent you use, you are going to cover the flowers with it. Cut the stems rather short on the flowers; then you won't need so much drying agent to cover them. Many stems become too weak to support their flowers after drying, anyway.

Material necessary for drying flowers by the silica gel method.

Stand the flowers in about one inch of silica gel.

Gradually cover the flowers with silica gel.

If you plan to make a bouquet, buy some florist's wire and run one piece up the center of the short stem remaining with the flower. The wire need not be covered by the drying agent. Later the wire can serve as an artificial stem in the bouquet.

If you are using silica gel as the drying agent, you will need a metal box—an old coffee can or a cookie tin—with a lid that fits tightly. Pour enough silica gel to make a layer about one inch deep. Now place one or a few flowers

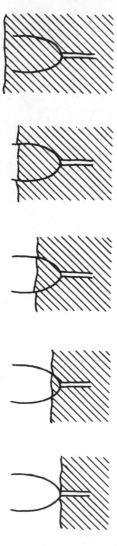

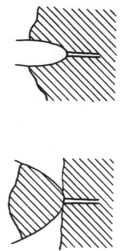

When drying cup-shaped flowers, be sure to add a little drying agent to the inside and a little to the outside. Then repeat this until the flower is covered. Try to keep the levels of the drying agent inside and outside the flowers nearly the same while you are doing this.

If you fill a cup-shaped flower with drying agent before adding any around the flower, the flower may spread open. If you put it around the flower before you put any in it, the flower may collapse inward.

on the silica gel. Most flowers should be dried right side up, or perhaps tilted a little to one side. If you used florist's wire, bend it any way you need to, to have it fit in the box. You can straighten it later. Some flat flowers, daisies for example, can be put in upside down.

Using your fingers or a tweezers, hold the flower in place and pour silica gel around it and on it. The silica gel must both support the flower and cover it. Pour a little to one side of the flower, then another side, and so on around it and on it. If the flower is cup-shaped—like a tulip—alternate pouring a little silica gel outside and inside. Continue until the flower is covered.

You must make your own decisions about how much to pour on each side and where to pour next. Pour so that the petals and other flower parts are not disturbed. Pouring too much in one place at one time will push the petals out of place.

You can dry several flowers in the same box at the same time, but they should not touch each other or the sides of the box. Each one should be completely covered by the silica gel. The box probably will hold fewer flowers than you think it will.

Be sure the flowers are covered completely.

Put the lid on the box and seal it with tape. Let the flowers dry for a few days.

Place the lid securely on the box and tape it shut. Most flowers will be dry in about three or four days. Delicate flowers with thin petals may take only two days, and those with thick petals may take longer.[1] At the end of this time, open the box and gently pour off the silica gel. Try to disturb the flowers as little as possible. Remember that dried flowers are very delicate and break easily. You must handle them very carefully and have a great deal of patience. If a few petals do break off, you may be able to put them back on with a very small drop of white glue.

Some particles of silica gel probably will stick to the flowers. Gently brush them off with a camel's hair brush. If you let any silica gel remain, it will absorb moisture from the air, and this will make spots on the flowers.

As they dry, flowers usually shrink, so you must expect them to be a little smaller than they were when you

[1] There are several books devoted entirely to the art of flower drying, and some of them have tables of drying times best for different kinds of flowers. One good book that gives drying times for the silica gel method is *The Decorative Art of Dried Flower Arrangement* by Georgia S. Vance (Doubleday & Company, Inc., 1972).

* 49 *

picked them. Their colors often change, too. Some colors may become more beautiful, a few less attractive.

You can now arrange the dry flowers in a bouquet or other floral arrangement. If necessary, bend the florist's wire back into a shape that looks natural for a stem. Some florists sell a green tape that you can wind around the wires to make them look more like stems. Another thing you can do is to use hollow stems of plants like grasses, goldenrods, and some others. Check the plants in your area for sturdy, hollow stems. Collect them in autumn when they are dry or collect them earlier and hang them up to dry at home. You can cut them to whatever lengths you need for your bouquet.

Dried flowers will keep for a long time in a dry climate. The more humid the air, the shorter the time they will look well. A hot, humid summer will damage them if you don't have air conditioning. If you want to store a bouquet, keep it in a box with a tight-fitting lid and put a little silica gel in the box to keep the air dry. It would be best to tape the box shut.

If you store individual flowers, be sure they are in an

upright position. For this, they will need support. You probably can think of several ways to do this with materials you have at home, but here are a few ideas:

You could pour a layer of sand in the bottom of the box and then stick the stems in the sand. The layer of sand should be deep enough to support the flowers well.

Turn a plastic berry box upside down, and stick the stems through the holes in the box.

If the flowers have very short stems, you can use the plastic trays on which meat is sold. Rest the flowers along the rim of the tray.

Whichever method you use, put the flowers in a sealed box along with some silica gel.

With repeated use, silica gel absorbs so much water from plants and from the air that it no longer is a good drying agent. Then you must dry it. Most silica gel contains small blue granules. When these blue granules fade, it is time to dry the silica gel. Put it in an *open* container and put this in an oven set at 250°F. When the granules are blue again—perhaps in two or three hours—the silica

After the silica gel has been poured off, the flowers can be stored on any convenient support. They should then be put along with some silica gel in a larger container that can be sealed.

gel is dry. Be sure to store it then in a tightly sealed container.

If you use the combined borax–cornmeal–salt mixture as your drying agent, you dry the plants the same way as with silica gel but you use a container with no lid. As the combined agent absorbs water from the flowers, the water in the agent evaporates into the air. With this method it takes about ten days for most flowers to dry.[2]

The combined agent works best in dry weather. In humid weather it may take much longer for the flowers to dry than in dry weather.

[2] *The Art of Drying Plants and Flowers* by Mabel Squires (Bonanza Books, 1968) has a table of drying times for the combined borax–cornmeal–salt mixture.

5

Pressing Fresh Plants

Pressing is one of the oldest means of preserving plants. The great botanical gardens all over the world have collections of millions of pressed plants.

When you gather plants for pressing, take only those that look fresh and healthy. Dry, brittle plants will crack when they are pressed. Don't take any that are covered by insects. Pressing will not kill all of them.

Because the specimens will be mounted later on sheets of paper, collect specimens that will fit on the paper you plan to use.

Press the plants soon after you arrive home. They should be pressed while they are still rather fresh. Badly wilted plants can be difficult to handle, but sometimes a slightly wilted plant is easier to arrange for pressing than is a very fresh, stiff one. If you can't attend to them immediately, keep them in the container in which you collected them and place it in a refrigerator. They probably will stay in good condition overnight.

Plants should be pressed between newspapers. Lay each specimen flat on a newspaper and fold the newspaper over. If the specimens are wet, pat them dry with paper towels. You can put several small specimens in each folded sheet, but lay them next to each other—not one on top of the other.

If you collect twigs or branches with flowers, one specimen to a sheet probably is enough. Try to arrange the leaves and flowers so that they will look as natural as possible. It is a good idea, however, to twist one leaf over to show its lower surface.

Some plant parts are too thick to be pressed. Obviously, you cannot press an acorn. Keep dry fruits like this separately in boxes. Woody stems should not be pressed unless they are very slender.

Lay a specimen to be pressed on clean newspaper.

Fold the newspaper to cover the specimen.

If a stem is thick and fleshy, slice it down the center and throw one half away. Then press the remaining half with the cut side down. If the stem is very thick, you may have to cut away more than half.

Very small berries can be pressed. If a large, fleshy fruit contains no hard seeds—like a pepper—you can cut a very thin slice across the middle and press this. Juicy fruits are best not pressed, but some small ones can be hung up to dry.

If the specimen is longer than the paper you plan to mount it on, you can bend the stem into a V-shape or a Z-shape.

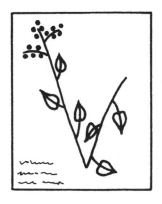

Add more newspapers above and below the one with the specimen.

Lay heavy books on the newspapers.

When you have the specimens arranged as you want them, make a pile of the folded newspaper sheets with the specimens inside them, but alternate these with several layers of other, empty newspapers. Each specimen should be separated from the next one by layers of newspapers at least a sixteenth of an inch thick. Keep the entire pile on a flat surface (a table or the floor), and then cover the pile with a large book (or a wooden board or very thick cardboard). Lay several large books or other heavy objects on top. Try to distribute them evenly over the pile so that all the plants receive equal pressure.

Let the plants stay like this for one day. During this time the newspapers will absorb some of the water from the plants. Then remove them from the newspaper and put them in fresh, dry newspapers just as you did the day before. By now the plants will have become limp, and you probably can change the positions of the leaves and flowers if you wish to do so. Later, as the plants become drier, it will become more difficult to do this.

Press the plants for another day. Remove them and place them in fresh newspaper for another two or three days. By this time most plants will be dry. If some of the material was originally thick and fleshy, you may have to change them every day for a week or more. In humid weather you will have to make more changes than in dry weather. The plants must be completely dry, otherwise they will become moldy.

When the plants are dry, you can mount them on paper. Professional botanists use a heavy paper about the size of a half page of newspaper, but you can mount your specimens on paper the size of typing paper. The paper should be quite heavy. A good quality of typing paper or mimeograph paper will do well for most of your specimens if you are careful not to collect large ones.

Using white glue, attach the specimens to the paper, one specimen to a sheet. If the specimen is small and simple, place glue on the back, and then lay the specimen on the paper. If it is somewhat larger and complicated, it may be difficult to turn over and lay down exactly as you want it. In this case, lay the specimen face down on some old newspaper and put glue on the back of the specimen. Then lay a clean sheet of good paper on the specimen and press

After the specimen has dried completely—which will be after several changes of newspapers—glue the specimen to a fresh sheet of paper.

Add the name of the plant and the place and date you collected it.

down on it. When you turn the paper over, the specimen should be attached to it. Add a little glue wherever it may be needed.

Spread the mounted sheets with their specimens on a table for a day or two until the glue dries. Then you can pile them up, but don't make the piles too high, or the bottom specimens will become crushed. Storing the piles in boxes will help to keep them neat, for they tend to slide.

A few small leaves or flowers may be pressed in a book. Be sure to put them inside newspaper first. Change the newspaper every day for a few days. Pressing many specimens or thick ones in a book is likely to ruin the book. So is pressing wet ones.

If you live in a large city, use an old telephone book. Damage to the book won't matter. If you put all the specimens near the back of the book, the weight of the rest of the book will be enough to press small specimens.

If you want to make flower "pictures" for framing, remove flowers and leaves from twigs and press them each separately. They should be small enough to fit inside the

Pressed plants framed to make decorations. LEFT: Four
ragweed leaves, three short stems of larch with their needles,
and two red clover heads. RIGHT: three foxtail grass stems,
three lady's thumb stems (with leaves and flowers), and two
red clover leaves.

frame you plan to use. Choose a piece of construction paper or cloth with a dull finish for the background. Avoid bright colors for they will detract from the color of the flowers. Cut one or two pieces of cardboard to fit inside the frame. The cardboard should be thick enough to hold the flowers in place when everything is assembled.

Place the paper or cloth on the cardboard and then arrange the pressed flowers and leaves on the paper or cloth to form the picture that you have in mind. Do not glue them in place. Lay the glass from the frame on the entire arrangement. Then put the frame over this and very carefully pick everything up and turn it over without letting anything slip. Put the back of the frame in place and secure it.

6

Collecting Live Plants

If you like gardening and have a place in which to garden, you might want to have a collection of living plants growing in your own yard.

When you collect plants for this purpose, choose only those plants that seem likely to be able to survive in your own garden. If you dig up ferns from deep inside a shady woods and plant them in a sunny garden with no shade, they probably will die. Plants taken from a sunny field will not do well if transplanted into a wooded area or the shady side of a house. A plant picked up on your vacation in southern Florida probably will die if you plant it in your backyard in Montana. It might not even survive the long trip to your home.

Many gardeners are tempted to transplant rare or endangered plants into their own gardens. Some persons do this because they enjoy having plants that their neighbors don't have. Others feel that by growing these plants they are helping to protect them. But many rare plants are rare because they need very special conditions to survive, and these special conditions are found in only one or a few places on earth. The Venus's-flytrap, for example, grows naturally only in a swampy area along the border between North Carolina and South Carolina. Here the summers are warm enough, and the winters are not too cold. The concentration of mineral nutrients in the soil is just right. Most person's backyards are not like that, and it would take a great deal of work to make them that way. Most Venus's-flytraps sold by nurseries die within a few months because few persons know how to take proper care of them. Instead of protecting endangered plants, these persons are killing them.

The best wild plants to start with in your garden are those that are rather common in your own part of the country. Many rather pretty wild flowers grow with such ease that they are considered to be weeds in some places. Violets, buttercups, butter-and-eggs, bouncing Bet, daisies, wild roses, sunfllowers, and bracken fern are a few examples. Most of them are pretty enough for any flower garden. Wild strawberries and red raspberries are delicious to eat as well.

Farmers consider most of these plants to be weeds in their fields, and many gardeners don't want them in their gardens if they are raising something else. You probably could get permission to dig up many of these plants from farms or a neighbor's garden.

Transplant at a time when there is the least danger of the plants drying out and wilting. An overcast day is good. A rainy day is even better, but don't get soaked yourself and catch a cold. On a sunny day try to do your transplanting in the evening. Then the plants can recover during the cool, damp night.

When choosing plants to transplant, select healthy-looking ones that are not infested with insects or fungi. You don't want to bring any pests into your garden.

Take along some kind of container in which to carry

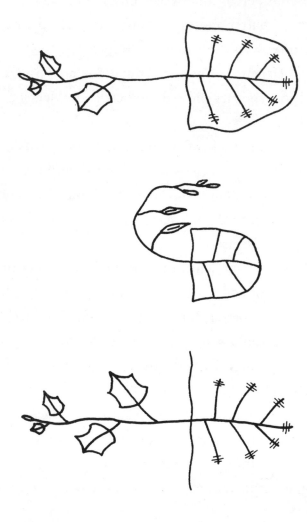

If you take only a small ball of soil when you dig up a plant you probably will cut off all or most of the root hairs. Then the plant will wilt and may even die. If you take a larger ball of soil, you are more likely to get all or most of the root hairs. It also helps to cut off a few of the lower leaves.

Dig a hole large enough to hold the ball of soil around the roots of the plant. Add water until the soil is soaked. Put the plant in the hole and add soil to fill in any spaces left over.

the plants. If your trip is to be a short one, a cardboard box will be fine, but if it is a long one, it would be a good idea to put a plastic bag around the roots as soon as you dig up the plant. This will help to keep the roots from drying out.

Be sure to dig up a large ball of soil with the roots. This way you will not be so likely to damage them. Most of the water absorbed by roots is taken in by the millions of very fine root hairs that grow a very short distance back from the root tips. If you cut off most of them the plant will not be able to absorb much water. Then it will almost certainly wilt badly and may even die before it can grow new ones.

If any of the leaves are dead or dying, pick them off immediately. These leaves are no longer of use to the plant, but water will evaporate from them. If the plant has many leaves, you might remove some of the lower ones even if they do look healthy; this helps to conserve water in the plant. A second plastic bag placed over the top of the plant will help, too.

When you get home, dig a hole large enough for the roots and the ball of soil around them. Fill the hole with water. If the soil is dry, the water will soak into it almost immediately. Keep filling the hole until the water level falls slowly. Then you are sure the ground is well soaked.

Remove any plastic bags from the plant and place the ball of soil with its roots into the hole. Fill in any space left over with soil and pack it down firmly. If the ball of soil around the roots has become dry, add just a little more water.

For a few days, check the plant every day to see if it needs water. If it still looks good four or five days after transplanting, it probably will survive. After that it will need watering only in dry weather.

Plants with *rhizomes* (underground stems) or bulbs usually are easy to transplant, because these parts contain a supply of stored food, and new roots sprout readily from most rhizomes and bulbs. Even if the plants do not grow as well the first year as you had hoped, as long as they have a good, thick rhizome or bulb, very likely they will survive the winter and do better next year.

Many violets have rhizomes. As the rhizomes grow, they branch, and the tip of each branch has a cluster of a

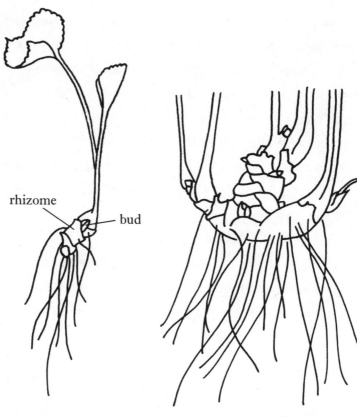

rhizome

bud

YOUNG VIOLET PLANT

**BRANCHED RHIZOME
OF OLDER PLANT**

few leaves. So each clump of violets will become thicker each year. You can dig these up and break them into several smaller plants and transplant them. Violets also produce seeds that they shoot a short distance. So in a year or two you may find new plants growing near the old ones.

Strawberries grow in much the same way, but they have *runners*, which are stems that grow along the surface of the ground. New plants grow from the runners. You can separate the young plants and transplant them.

Some plants are hard to transplant. Many vines, for instance, have such large root systems that it is almost impossible to dig up a ball of soil large enough to get all the roots unless the plant is very young. A ten-foot-tall sunflower plant would be difficult to transplant, too. You could collect some of these plants by gathering their seeds and planting them. Each seed contains one living embryonic plant within it.

Collect the seeds when they are ripe. That's usually in autumn. Because some seeds must have cold weather before they will germinate, the simplest thing to do would be to plant them right away and let them spend the winter outdoors. Just scatter them on the soil in the garden. Cover them with a thin layer of soil and then with some of the leaves that are falling from the trees at this time of year. Don't plant them deeply in the soil, especially if they are small seeds. In nature very few seeds are actually planted.

Don't be surprised if only a few of these wild seeds germinate next year. Our garden plants have been bred so that their seeds germinate as soon as we plant them in spring. In fact, some of them die when they are only two or three years old. In nature, seeds of many plants will live for many years, and some will come up one year, some the next year, and some in the following years. This helps them to survive a flood, a drought, or other catastrophe. Even if all the plants that come up one year are killed, the seeds remaining in the soil might survive and germinate the next year.

If you started a dry seed or fruit collection, as suggested in Chapter Three, you might find that the seeds are still alive even though they may be several years old.

7

Photographing Plants

One of the best ways to collect plants is by taking pictures of them. This is especially true of endangered plants, for you don't have to pick them to photograph them. Do try, however, not to trample a hundred plants in your eagerness to get to the one that looks best to you. Photography is also good for plants or plant parts that are too tall, too thick, too juicy, or too hard for making leaf prints, for drying, or for pressing. You can photograph plants in their natural environment. In other methods of collecting you remove them from where they grow.

This book does not give you directions on how to operate your camera. Each camera comes with its own directions. If you buy special accessories for it, they will come with their own directions, too. There are a few tips that you might find helpful, however.

You must, of course, focus carefully. If not, your subject will appear fuzzy in the picture. If the directions for your equipment say that it will not focus any closer than four feet, then don't come any closer than four feet. If you do, the only thing that might be in focus is something in the background.

Red raspberry leaves in focus.

The photographer focussed the camera too far away to get
the red raspberry leaves in focus. The violet leaves to the right
of the picture are nearer the ground and they are in focus, but
they are not the intended subject of the picture.

In one way, taking pictures of plants is easier than
taking pictures of animals. Plants don't run away. But on
windy days, branches don't stand still either. If they move,
they are likely to appear blurred in the picture. If you are
going to take close-ups of flowers or other plant parts,
try to do it on a calm day. On windy days there sometimes
are pauses between breezes, and you will have to wait for

The photographer moved the camera as the picture was taken. Everything is fuzzy.

them. You must be ready to snap a picture quickly during a pause.

No matter how quickly you must take a picture, be sure you hold the camera steady while you are taking it. Otherwise everything in the picture will be blurred.

In spite of what many people think, you do not have to take pictures only on a sunny day to get good results. This is especially true of color film.

Spots of sunshine and shade on the subject of your

photograph can detract from it. For this reason, pictures of plants in a woods often look better if they are taken on cloudy days. Here is one hint about taking pictures on overcast days. Try to arrange your picture so that the sky is not at the upper edge of the picture. One way you can do this is by pointing the camera downward toward a flower so that there is no sky in the picture at all. Another way is

Violet leaves in bright sunlight. The picture is more pleasing than the one taken in mixed sun and shade.

Violet leaves under a tree on a sunny day. The shadows of the tree's branches mixed with the sunlight that passes between them make this picture rather unattractive.

Violet leaves on a cloudy day. This picture is also more attractive than the one taken in mixed sun and shade.

to see that something—perhaps the branch of a tree—is at the top of the picture. This helps to frame the picture, too.

Plants growing along a roadside are often covered with dust from the passing traffic. If you walk ten or twenty feet back from the road you might find the same kind of plant looking much cleaner and fresher.

Try not to have a cluttered background. See if aiming your camera from a different angle will change the background. If this does not work, you might try standing a large piece of posterboard behind the plant to use as a background. You may need a friend to hold it in place. Some photographers who use color film use sky-blue posterboard so that the artificial background looks like real sky. If you use black and white film the exact color does not matter so much. A dark background would be best for light-colored flowers, and a light background would be good for dark flowers.

Before you snap a picture, check to be sure that there isn't something in the picture that you don't want there. It is very discouraging to find later that you have a photograph of a beautiful plant with a crumpled newspaper or an old pop bottle in the foreground.

Here are some ideas for plant photographs. For very small subjects you will need close-up attachments or extension tubes (or bellows), but for larger subjects just an inexpensive camera in good working condition is fine.

1. Individual flowers or clusters of flowers.

2. Individual fruits or seeds.

3. Leaf types. See Chapter One for some examples.

4. Shapes of trees. Take silhouettes of trees against the sky. If a tree drops its leaves in autumn, take the same tree in summer and winter.

5. Patterns—like the patterns formed by ivy leaves on a wall, by the little florets in a big sunflower head, or by the bark on a tree.

6. Changing seasons. Follow a tree or shrub (or a woods or field) through all the seasons of the year.

7. Different ecological settings. Depending on where you live, you might photograph the plants growing in woods, meadows, seashores, mountaintops, riverbanks, swamps, abandoned farms, roadsides, vacant lots, sandy places, rocky places, muddy places—in fact, anywhere. Vacation trips will give you opportunities to add to this collection.

8. Autumn colors of trees and shrubs. You'll need color film for this.

9. Anything else about plants that interests you.